MW01616566

0

Enjoy all our books for free…

Interesting biographies, engaging introductions, and more.
Join the exclusive United Library reviewers club!
You will get a new book delivered in your inbox every Friday.

Join us today, go to: https://campsite.bio/unitedlibrary

Introduction

Aristotle (c. 384 B.C. to 322 B.C.) was an Ancient Greek philosopher and scientist who is still considered one of the greatest thinkers in politics, psychology and ethics. When Aristotle turned 17, he enrolled in Plato's Academy.

In 335, Aristotle founded his own school, the Lyceum, in Athens, where he spent most of the rest of his life studying, teaching and writing.

Some of his most notable works include *Nichomachean Ethics*, *Politics*, *Metaphysics*, *Poetics* and *Prior analytics*.

In 338, Aristotle began tutoring Alexander the Great.

"Knowing yourself is the beginning of all wisdom." - Aristoteles

This is the descriptive, concise biography of Aristotle.

Table of Contents

Aristotle

Aristotle (* 384 BC in Stageira; † 322 BC in Chalcis on Euboea) was a Greek polymath. He is one of the most famous and influential philosophers and naturalists in history.

His teacher was Plato, but Aristotle either founded or significantly influenced numerous disciplines, including philosophy of science, philosophy of nature, logic, biology, physics, ethics, theory of government, and theory of poetry. Aristotelianism developed from his thought.

Fact: Aristotle was born in Greece in 384 BC. He was nobility as his father Nicomachus served as a physician in the court of King Amyntus III of Macedonia. His parents passed away while he was a young boy. Aristotle's older sister, Arimneste and her husband Proxenus of Atarneus, became Aristotle's guardian until he came of age.

Overview

Life

Aristotle, who came from a family of physicians, arrived in Athens at the age of seventeen. In 367 BC, he joined Plato's Academy. There he participated in research and teaching. After Plato's death, he left Athens in 347.

In 343/342 he became the teacher of Alexander the Great, the heir to the throne in the Kingdom of Macedonia. In 335/334 he returned to Athens. He was no longer a member of the Academy, but taught and researched independently with his students in the Lykeion. In 323/322 he had to leave Athens again because of political tensions and went to Chalkis, where he died soon after.

Plant

Aristotle's writings in dialogue form, addressed to a general public, are lost. The surviving doctrinal writings were for the most part intended only for internal classroom use and were continuously edited. Subject areas are:

Logic, philosophy of science, rhetoric: In the logical writings, Aristotle elaborates a theory of argumentation (dialectic) on the basis of discussion practices in the academy and establishes formal logic with the syllogistic. On the basis of his syllogistics, he elaborates a philosophy of science and makes significant contributions to the theory of definition and the theory of meaning, among other things. He describes rhetoric as the art of proving statements to be plausible, thus bringing it close to logic.

Theory of nature: Aristotle's philosophy of nature addresses the fundamentals of every view of nature: the types and principles of change. He meets the then current question of how coming into being and passing away is possible with the help of his well-known distinction between form and matter: the same matter can take on different forms.

In his scientific works, he also examines the parts and behaviors of animals as well as humans and their functions. In his theory of the soul - in which "to be animate" means "to be alive" - he argues that the soul, which constitutes the various vital functions of living beings, belongs to the body as its form. However, he also conducted empirical research and made significant contributions to zoological biology.

Metaphysics: In his Metaphysics Aristotle argues (against Plato's assumption of abstract entities) at first for the fact that the concrete single things (like Socrates) are the substances, i.e. the fundamental of all reality. He supplements this with his later teaching, according to which the substance of concrete individual things is their form.

Ethics and state theory: The goal of human life, according to Aristotle in his Ethics, is the good life, happiness. For a happy life, one must form virtues of intellect and (through education and habituation) virtues of character, which includes appropriate handling of desires and emotions.

His political philosophy follows on from ethics. According to this, the state as a form of community is a prerequisite for human happiness. Aristotle asks about the conditions of happiness and compares different constitutions for this purpose. The doctrine of the state that he developed enjoyed unchallenged authority for many centuries.

Theory of poetry: In his theory of poetry, Aristotle deals in particular with tragedy, whose function, in his view, is to arouse fear and pity in order to bring about a purification of these emotions in the spectator *(catharsis).*

Aftermath

Aristotle's scientific research program was continued after his death by his collaborator Theophrastus, who also founded the Aristotelian school, the Peripatos, in the legal sense. Aristotle's commentary did not begin until the 1st century B.C.E. and was pursued in particular by Platonists. Through the mediation of Porphyrios and Boethius, Aristotelian logic became seminal for the Latin-speaking Middle Ages. From the 12th/13th century on, all of Aristotle's fundamental works were available in Latin translation. They were authoritative for scholasticism until the early modern period.

The examination of Aristotle's theory of nature shaped the natural sciences of the late Middle Ages and the Renaissance. In the Arabic-speaking world, Aristotle was the most intensively received ancient author in the Middle Ages. His work has shaped intellectual history in many ways; important distinctions and concepts such as "substance," "accident," "matter," "form," "energy," "potency," "category," "theory," and "practice" go back to Aristotle.

Life

Aristotle was born in 384 BC in Stageira, an independent Ionian town on the east coast of Chalkidiki. Therefore he is sometimes called "the Stagirite". His father Nikomachos was personal physician to King Amyntas III of Macedonia, and his mother Phaestis came from a family of physicians from Chalkis on Euboia. Nicomachus died before Aristotle came of age. Proxenos from Atarneus was appointed guardian.

First stay in Athens

In 367 BC, Aristotle arrived in Athens at the age of seventeen and entered Plato's Academy. There he was initially engaged in the mathematical and dialectical subjects that formed the beginning of studies in the Academy. Early on he began to write works, including dialogues modeled on those of Plato. He also studied contemporary rhetoric, especially the teaching of the orator Isocrates. Against the pedagogical concept of Isocrates, which aimed at immediate benefit, he defended the Platonic educational ideal of the philosophical training of thought.

He took up a teaching position at the Academy. In this context, the oldest of his surviving doctrinal writings were produced as lecture manuscripts, including the logical writings, which were later summarized under the name *Organon* ("tool"). Some passages of the text indicate that the lecture hall was decorated with paintings depicting scenes from the life of Plato's teacher Socrates.

Travel years

"Adventure is worthwhile" - Aristoteles

After Plato's death, Aristotle left Athens in 347 BC. Possibly he did not agree with Plato's nephew Speusippos taking over the leadership of the Academy; moreover, he had run into political difficulties.

In 348 BC, King Philip II of Macedonia had conquered Chalcidice, destroyed Olynthos, and also captured Aristotle's hometown of Stageira. This campaign was recognized by the anti-Macedonian party in Athens as a grave threat to Athenian independence. Because of the traditional ties of Aristotle's family to the Macedonian court, anti-Macedonian sentiment was also directed against him. Since he was not an Athenian citizen, but only a metoe of dubious loyalty, his position in the city was relatively weak.

He accepted an invitation from Hermias, who ruled the cities of Assos and Atarneus on the Asia Minor coast opposite the island of Lesbos. To secure his domain against the Persians, Hermias was allied with Macedonia. Other philosophers also found refuge in Assos. The very controversial Hermias is described by the tradition friendly to him as a wise and heroic philosopher, but by the opposing one as a tyrant. Aristotle, who was a friend of Hermias, initially stayed in Assos; in 345/344 BC he moved to Mytilene on Lesbos. There he collaborated with his student Theophrastos, a native of Lesbos, who shared his interest in biology. Later, both went to Stageira.

In 343/342 B.C., Aristotle went to Mieza at the invitation of Philip II to instruct his then thirteen-year-old son Alexander (later called "the Great"). The instruction ended no later than 340/339 BC, when Alexander took over the regency for his absent father.

Aristotle had a copy of the Iliad made for Alexander, which the king, as an admirer of Achilles, later carried with him on his conquests. The relationship between teacher and pupil has not been handed down in detail; it has given rise to legends and many speculations. It is certain that their political convictions were fundamentally different; in any case, an influence of Aristotle on Alexander is not recognizable. Aristotle, however, is said to have achieved the reconstruction of his destroyed hometown Stageira at the Macedonian court; the credibility of this news, however, is doubtful.

The execution of Hermias by the Persians in 341/340 touched Aristotle deeply, as a poem dedicated to the memory of his friend shows.

When after the death of Speusippos in 339/338 B.C. the office of the scholar (principal) became vacant in the academy, Aristotle could not participate in the election of the successor only because of his absence; however, he was still considered an academy member. Later, he went to Delphi with his great-nephew, the historian Kallisthenes, to prepare a list of winners of the Pythian Games on behalf of the amphictyons there.

Second stay in Athens

With the destruction of the rebellious city of Thebes in 335 BC, the open resistance against the Macedonians in Greece collapsed, and in Athens, too, people came to terms with the balance of power. Therefore, Aristotle was able to return to Athens in 335/334 B.C. and began to research and teach there again, but was now no longer active at the Academy, but in a public gymnasium, the Lykeion. Here he created his own school, the direction of which was taken over by Theophrastos after his death. New excavations may have made it possible to identify the building complex

In the legal sense, however, it was Theophrastus who founded the school and acquired the property - the later common designations Peripatos and Peripatetics specifically for this school are not yet attested for the time of Theophrastus. The wealth of material that Aristotle collected (on the 158 constitutions of the Greek city-states, for example) suggests that he had numerous collaborators who did research outside Athens. He was wealthy and owned a large library. His relationship with the Macedonian governor Antipater was friendly.

Retreat from Athens, death and descendants

After the death of Alexander the Great in 323 BC, anti-Macedonian forces initially prevailed in Athens and other Greek cities. Delphi revoked an honorary decree awarded to Aristotle. Hostilities arose in Athens that made it impossible for him to continue working quietly. Therefore, he left Athens in 323/322 BC. Allegedly, he expressed on this occasion that he did not want the Athenians to transgress against philosophy a second time (after they had already sentenced Socrates to death). He retired to Chalkis on Euboia to his mother's house. There he died in October 322 BC.

Aristotle was married to Pythias, a relative of his friend Hermias. From her he had a daughter, also named Pythias. After the death of his wife, Herpyllis, who was of low origin, became his companion; she may have been the mother of his son Nicomachus. In his will, the execution of which he entrusted to Antipater, Aristotle regulated, among other things, the future marriage of his daughter, who was still a minor, and made provisions for the material security of Herpyllis.

Plant

Note: References from works of Aristotle are given as follows: Title citation (abbreviations are resolved by link at the first position in the chapter) and, where appropriate, book and chapter citation and Bekker number. The Bekker number indicates an exact location in the corpus. It is noted in good modern editions.

Due to breaks and inconsistencies in Aristotle's work, research has moved away from the previously widespread idea that the surviving work forms a closed, through-composed system. These breaks are probably due to developments, changes of perspective, and different emphases in different contexts. Since a secure chronological order of his writings cannot be determined, statements about Aristotle's actual development remain conjectures. Although his work does not *de facto* form a finished system, his philosophy possesses characteristics of a *potential* system.

Tradition and character of the writings

"To write well, express yourself like the common people, but think like a wise man." - Aristoteles

Various ancient directories attribute nearly 200 titles to Aristotle. If Diogenes Laertios' figure is correct, Aristotle left behind a life's work of over 445,270 lines (although this figure probably does not include two of the most extensive writings - the *Metaphysics* and the

Nicomachean Ethics). Only about a quarter of it has survived.

In research, two groups are distinguished: *exoteric* writings (which were published for a wider audience) and *esoteric* (which served for the internal use of the school). All exoteric writings do not exist or exist only in fragments, while most esoteric ones have survived. The writing The *Constitution of the Athenians* was considered lost and was only found in papyrus form at the end of the 19th century.

Exoteric and esoteric writings

The exoteric writings consisted mainly of dialogues in the tradition of Plato, e.g. the *Protreptikos* - a promotional writing for philosophy -, investigations such as *On the Ideas,* but also propaedeutic collections. Cicero praises their "golden flow of speech."

The esoteric writings, also called pragmatics, have often been described as lecture manuscripts; this is not certain and for some writings or sections also unlikely. It is widely believed that they grew out of the teaching activity. Large parts of the Pragmatia show a peculiar style full of omissions, allusions, leaps of thought, and doublets.

In addition, however, there are stylistically sophisticated passages that make it clear (along with the duplicates) that Aristotle worked repeatedly on his texts, and suggest the possibility that he was thinking of publishing at least some of the Pragmatia. Aristotle assumes great prior knowledge of foreign texts and theories on the part of his addressees.

16

References to the exoteric writings show that their knowledge is also assumed.

The Manuscripts of Aristotle

After Aristotle's death, his manuscripts initially remained in the possession of his students. When his student and successor Theophrast died, his student Neleus is said to have received Aristotle's library and to have left Athens with it - out of anger at not having been elected successor - with some followers in the direction of Skepsis near Troy in Asia Minor.

The ancient reports mention an adventurous and dubious story, according to which the heirs of Neleus buried the manuscripts in the cellar to secure them from foreign access, where they then remained lost.

It is largely certain that in the first century BC Apellikon of Teos acquired the damaged manuscripts and brought them to Athens, and that they reached Rome after Sulla's conquest of Athens in 86 BC. The latter's son commissioned Tyrannion in the middle of the century to sift through the manuscripts and supplement them with further material.

Other ways of transmission

Even if Aristotle's manuscripts were lost for centuries with his library, it is undisputed that his teachings were at least partially known in Hellenism, especially through the exoteric writings and indirectly probably also through Theophrast's work. In addition, some pragmatics must have been known, of which there were possibly copies in the library of Peripatos.

Andronikos of Rhodes. The first edition

On the basis of Tyrannion's work, his student Andronikos of Rhodes, in the second half of the first century BC, provided the first edition of Aristotle's Pragmatia, which was probably only partly based on Aristotle's manuscripts. The writings of this edition constitute the Corpus Aristotelicum. Presumably, some compilations of previously unordered books as well as some titles go back to this edition.

It is possible that Andronikos also made interventions in the text - such as cross-references. In the case of the numerous doublets, he may have arranged different texts on the same subject one after the other. The present arrangement of the writings largely corresponds to this edition. Andronikos did not take into account the exoteric writings that were still available at his time. They were lost in the following period.

Manuscripts and printed editions

Today's editions are based on copies dating back to the Andronikos edition. With over 1000 manuscripts, Aristotle is the most widely distributed among non-Christian Greek-language authors. The oldest manuscripts date from the 9th century. Because of its size, the Corpus Aristotelicum is never completely contained in a single codex.

After the invention of printing, the first printed edition from the hand of Aldus Manutius appeared in 1495-1498. The complete edition of the Berlin Academy, edited by Immanuel Bekker in 1831, is the basis of modern Aristotle research. It is based on collations of the best manuscripts available at the time. According to its page, column and line count (Bekker count), Aristotle is still quoted everywhere today. For a few works, it still provides the authoritative text; most, however, are now available in new individual editions.

Classification of sciences and basic

Aristotle's work covers large parts of the knowledge available at his time. He divides it into three areas:

- theoretical science
- practical science
- poietic science

Theoretical knowledge is sought for its own sake. Practical and poietic knowledge has another purpose, the (good) action or a (beautiful or useful) work. According to the nature of the objects, he further subdivides theoretical knowledge: (i) First Philosophy ("metaphysics") treats (with the theory of substance, the theory of principle, and theology) the independent and the immutable, (ii) natural science treats the independent and the mutable, and (iii) mathematics treats the independent and the immutable (Met. VI 1).

A special position seems to have the writings that do not appear in this classification, which were compiled only after the death of Aristotle in the so-called *Organon.*

The most important fonts can be roughly divided as follows:

For Aristotle, this division of the sciences is accompanied by the insight that each science also has its own principles due to its peculiar objects. Thus, there cannot be the same precision in practical science - the field of actions - as in the field of theoretical sciences. A science of ethics is possible, but its propositions are valid only as a rule.

Nor can this science prescribe the right course of action for all possible situations. Rather, ethics can only provide a non-exact knowledge in outline, which, moreover, alone does not enable a successful conduct of life, but for this must be connected to experiences and existing attitudes (EN I 1 1094b12-23).

Aristotle was convinced that "men are by nature sufficiently endowed for the true" (Rhet. I 1, 1355a15-17). Therefore, he typically first goes through (generally or with predecessors) accepted opinions *(endoxa)* and discusses their main problems *(aporiai) in order* to analyze a possible true core of these opinions (EN VII 2). Striking is his preference to lay the foundation for the argumentation in an all-statement at the beginning of a writing and to stake out the specific subject.

Language, logic and knowledge

"It is the mark of an educated mind to be able to entertain a thought without accepting it." - Aristoteles

The Organon

The subject area of language, logic and knowledge is dealt with mainly in the writings traditionally compiled under the title *Organon* (Greek: tool, method). This compilation and its title do not originate from Aristotle, and the order is not chronological. The text *Rhetoric does* not belong to the *Organon*, but is very close to it in content because of its way of treating the subject matter. One justification for the compilation is the common methodological-propaedeutic character.

Meaning Theory

In the following passage - considered the most influential text in the history of semantics - Aristotle distinguishes four elements that stand in two different relations to each other, a mapping relation and a symbol relation:

Thus, spoken and written words are different among people; written words symbolize spoken words. Mental experiences and the things are the same with all people; mental experiences represent the things. According to this, the relation of speech and writing to things is determined by agreement, whereas the relation of mental impressions to things is natural.

Truth and falsity come only to the connection and separation of *several* ideas. Also the single words do not establish a connection yet and therefore cannot be true or false ever alone. Therefore, only the whole proposition *(logos apophantikos)* can be true or false.

Predicates and properties

Some linguistic-logical observations are fundamental for Aristotle's philosophy and play an important role also outside the (in a broader sense) logical writings. In particular, this concerns the relation between predicates and (essential) properties.

Definitions

By a definition Aristotle primarily does not understand a nominal definition (which he also knows; see An. Post. II, 8-10), but a real definition. A nominal definition gives only opinions, which are connected with a name. What underlies these opinions in the world is given by the real definition: a definition of X gives necessary properties of X and what it means to be an X: the essence.

Possible object of a definition is with it (only) that what shows a (universal) being, in particular species like *man*. A species is defined by the specification of a (logical) genus and the species-forming difference. Thus, *man* can be defined as a *rational* (difference) *living being* (genus).

Individuals can therefore not be captured by definition, but only assigned to their respective species.

Categories as statement classes

Aristotle teaches that there are ten non-reducible propositions that answer the questions *What is X?, What is the nature of X?, Where is X?* etc. (→ the complete list). The categories have both a linguistic-logical and an ontological function, because predicates are stated by an underlying subject *(hypokeimenon)* (e.g. Socrates) on the one hand, and properties are attributed to it on the other (e.g.: white, human).

Accordingly, the categories represent the most general classes of both predicates and being. Aristotle distinguishes the category of substance, which contains

23

necessary, essential predicates, from the others, which contain accidental predicates.

When one predicates (states) of Socrates *man,* it is an essential statement that states of the subject (Socrates) *what* he is, that is, names the substance. This is obviously different from a statement like Socrates *is in the marketplace,* by which one specifies something accidental, namely *where* Socrates is (i.e. names the place).

Deduction and induction: argument types and means of cognition

Aristotle distinguishes two types of arguments or means of knowledge: Deduction *(syllogismos)* and Induction *(epagôgê).* The correspondence with the modern terms deduction and induction is extensive, but not complete. Deductions and inductions play central roles in various areas of Aristotelian argumentation theory and logic. Both originate in dialectics.

Deduction

According to Aristotle, a deduction consists of premises (assumptions) and a conclusion that is different from them. The conclusion follows with necessity from the premises. It cannot be false if the premises are true.

The definition of deduction *(syllogismos)* is thus broader than that of deduction (discussed below) - traditionally called syllogism - which consists of two premises and three terms. Aristotle distinguishes dialectical, eristic, rhetorical, and demonstrative deductions. These forms differ mainly according to the nature of their premises.

Induction

Aristotle explicitly contrasts deduction with induction; however, its determination and function is not as clear as that of deduction.

Aristotle is clear that such a transition from singular to general propositions is not logically valid without further conditions (An. Post. II 5, 91b34 f.). Corresponding conditions are met, for example, in the original, argumentation-logical context of dialectic, since the opponent must accept a general proposition introduced by induction if he cannot give a counterexample.

Above all, however, induction has the function of making the general *clear in* other, non-conclusive contexts by citing individual cases - be it as a didactic, be it as a heuristic procedure. Such induction provides plausible reasons for holding a general proposition to be true. Aristotle, however, nowhere inductively justifies the truth of such a proposition without further conditions.

Dialectics: theory of argumentation

The dialectic treated in the *topics* is a form of argumentation that (according to its genuine basic form) takes place in a dialogical disputation. It probably goes back to practices in Plato's Academy. The objective of the dialectic is:

Accordingly, the dialectic has no particular subject area, but can be applied universally. Aristotle determines the dialectic by the nature of the premises of this deduction. Its premises are recognized opinions *(endoxa).*

For dialectical premises it is irrelevant whether they are true or not. But why *recognized* opinions? In its basic form, dialectics takes place in an argumentative contest between two opponents with precisely assigned roles. To a presented problem of the form 'Is S P or not?' the answerer must commit himself to one of the two possibilities as thesis.

The dialectic conversation now consists of a questioner presenting statements to the answerer, which the latter must either affirm or deny. The answered questions are considered as premises. The goal of the questioner is now to form a deduction with the help of the affirmed or denied statements, so that the conclusion refutes the initial thesis

26

or something absurd or a contradiction follows from the premises. The method of dialectics has two components:

1. find out which premises give an argument for the sought conclusion.
2. find out which premises the answerer accepts.

For 2. the different types (a)-(ciii) of *recognized* opinions offer the questioner clues as to which questions the respective answerer will answer in the affirmative, that is, which premises he can use. Aristotle calls for lists of such recognized opinions (Top. I 14). Presumably he means lists separated according to the groups (a)-(ciii); these, in turn, are arranged according to points of view.

For 1. the instrument of toposes helps the dialectician in his argumentation construction. A topos is a construction guide for dialectical arguments, i.e. for finding suitable premises for a given conclusion. Aristotle lists about 300 of these toposes in the *Topics.* The dialectician knows these tops by heart, which can be ordered on the basis of their properties. The basis of this order is the system of predicates.

According to Aristotle, dialectic is useful for three things: (1) as an exercise, (2) for meeting the crowd, and (3) for philosophy. In addition to (1) the basic form of argumentative contest (in which there is a jury and rules and which probably goes back to practices in the academy), there are with (2) also modes of application that are dialogical but not rule-based contest, and with (3) those that are not dialogical but in which the dialectician in thought experiment (a) goes through difficulties on both sides (*diaporêsai*) or also (b) examines principles

(Top. I 4). For him, however, dialectic is not *the* method of philosophy or a fundamental science as it is for Plato.

"Not to know of what things one should demand demonstration, and of what one should not, argues want of education." - Aristoteles

Rhetoric: Theory of Persuasion

Aristotle defines rhetoric as "the ability to consider what is possibly persuasive *(pithanon) in* any matter" (Rhetoric I 2, 1355b26 f.). He calls it a counterpart *(antistrophos)* to dialectic. For, like dialectic, rhetoric is without delimited subject matter, and it uses the same elements (such as tops, recognized opinions, and especially deductions), and persuasion based on rhetorical deductions corresponds to dialectical reasoning.

Rhetoric was of outstanding importance in fourth-century democratic Athens, especially in the popular assembly and the courts, which were staffed by lay judges chosen by lot. Teachers of rhetoric were numerous, and manuals of rhetoric began to appear.

Aristotle's dialectical rhetoric is a reaction to the rhetorical theory of his time, which he criticizes as providing mere set pieces for speech situations and instructions on how to cloud the judgment of judges through slander and the arousal of emotion.

In contrast, his dialectical rhetoric is based on the view that we are most convinced when we think that something has been proven (Rhet. I 1, 1355a5 f.). That rhetoric is fact-oriented and must discover and exploit the potential for persuasion inherent in each case is also expressed by him in the weighting of the three means of persuasion. These are:

- the character of the speaker (ethos)

- the emotional state of the listener (pathos)

- the argument (logos)

He considers the argument to be the most important tool.

Among arguments, Aristotle distinguishes the example - a form of induction - and the enthymeme - a rhetorical deduction (again, the enthymeme is more important than the example). The enthymeme is a type of dialectical deduction. Its distinctive feature, due to the rhetorical situation, is that its premises are only *the* accepted opinions believed to be true by *all* or *most*. (The widespread, curious view that the enthymeme is a syllogism in which one of the two premises is missing is *not* held by Aristotle; it is based on a misunderstanding already attested in the ancient commentary of 1357a7 ff.) Accordingly, the speaker convinces the audience by deriving an assertion (as a conclusion) from the beliefs (as premises) of the audience.

The construction guides of these enthymemes provide rhetorical tops, e.g.:

Aristotle criticized contemporary teachers of rhetoric for neglecting argumentation and aiming exclusively at arousing emotion, for example, through behaviors such as whining or bringing the family to the court hearing, which prevented judges from making fact-based judgments.

According to Aristotle's theory, all emotions can be defined by considering three factors. One asks: (1) about what, (2) toward whom, and (3) in what state does someone feel the particular emotion? This is the definition of anger:

If the speaker can use this definitional knowledge to make it clear to the listeners that the corresponding state of affairs exists and that they are in the corresponding state of affairs, they feel the corresponding emotion. Insofar as the speaker uses this method to emphasize existing facts of a case, he does not thereby distract from the matter at hand - as was the case with the criticized predecessors - but only promotes emotions appropriate to the case and thus prevents inappropriate ones.Finally, the character of the speaker should appear credible, that is, virtuous, prudent and benevolent, to the listeners on the *basis of his speech* (Rhet. I 2, 1356a5-11; II 1, 1378a6-16)

The linguistic form also serves an argumentative-subject-oriented rhetoric. Aristotle, in fact, defines the optimal form *(aretê)* by being primarily clear, yet neither banal nor too sublime (Rhet. III 2, 1404b1-4). Through such balance, it promotes interest, attention, and understanding, and has a pleasing effect. Among the stylistic devices, metaphor in particular fulfills these conditions.

Syllogistic logic

If Aristotle's dialectical logic consists in a method of consistent reasoning, his syllogistic consists in a theory of reasoning itself. In the syllogistic he founded, Aristotle shows which conclusions are valid. For this he uses a form which in tradition is called simply *syllogism* (the Latin translation of *syllogismos*) because of the importance of this logic. Every syllogism is a (special form of) deduction *(syllogismos)*, but not every deduction is a syllogism (and this is because Aristotle's very general definition of deduction describes many possible argument types). Aristotle himself also does not use a separate term to distinguish the syllogism from other deductions.

A syllogism is a special deduction consisting of exactly two premises and one conclusion. Premises and conclusion together have exactly three different terms, terms (represented in the table by A, B, C). The premises have exactly one term in common (in the table B), which does not occur in the conclusion.

By the position of the common term, the middle term (here always B) Aristotle distinguishes the following syllogistic figures:

A predicate (P) (e.g. 'mortal') can be either ascribed or denied to a subject (S) (e.g. 'Greek'). This can be done in particular or in general form. Thus there are four forms in which S and P can be connected, as the following table shows (after *De interpretatione* 7; the vowels have been used since the Middle Ages for the particular type of statement and also in syllogistic).

The syllogism uses exactly these four types of statements in the following form:

Aristotle examines the following question: Which of the 192 possible combinations are logically valid deductions? In which syllogisms is it not possible that, if the premises are true, the conclusion is false? He distinguishes perfect syllogisms, which are immediately obvious, from imperfect ones. The imperfect syllogisms he traces back to the perfect ones by means of conversion rules (this procedure he calls *analysis*) or proves them indirectly.

A perfect syllogism is the - since the Middle Ages so called - *Barbara:*

For more valid syllogisms and their proofs, see the article Syllogism.

Aristotle applies the syllogistic elaborated in the *Analytica Priora in* his philosophy of science, the *Analytica Posteriora.*

Aristotle also develops a modal syllogistic that includes the terms *possible* and *necessary*. This modal syllogistic is much more difficult to interpret than the simple syllogistic. Whether a consistent interpretation of this modal syllogistic is possible at all is still controversial today. Interpretationally problematic, but also significant is Aristotle's definition of *possible*. He distinguishes the so-called one-sided and the two-sided possibility:

1. One-sided: p is possible insofar as non-p is not necessary.

2. Two-sided: p is possible if p is not necessary *and* not-p is not necessary, that is, p is contingent.

Thus, the indeterminism that Aristotle advocates can be characterized as the state that is contingent.

Canonical sentences

In Aristotelian logic, a distinction is made between the following contrary and adversative types of sentences - F and G stand for subject and predicate:

These "canonical theorems" are part of the foundation of traditional logic and are applied, among other things, in the case of simple or restricted conversion.

Knowledge and science

"Philosophy is the science which considers truth." - Aristoteles

Levels of knowledge

Aristotle distinguishes different stages of knowledge, which can be presented as follows (Met. I 1; An. post. II 19):

With this gradation, Aristotle also describes how knowledge arises: From perception memory arises and from memory by bundling of memory contents experience arises. Experience consists in a knowledge of a plurality of concrete individual cases and indicates only that, is mere factual knowledge. Knowledge, on the other hand (or science; *epistêmê* includes both), differs from experience in that it is

1. is general;

2. states not only the *that of* a fact, but also the *why,* the reason, or the explanatory cause.

In this process of knowledge, according to Aristotle, we advance from that which is more familiar to *us* and closer to sensory perception to that which is *intrinsically* or *inherently* more familiar, the principles and causes of things. That knowledge is supreme and superior does not mean, however, that in the concrete case it contains the other stages in the sense that it supersedes them. In action, moreover, experience as knowledge of the individual is sometimes superior to forms of knowledge that go to the general (Met. 981a12-25).

Causes and demonstrations

By a cause *(aitia)* Aristotle generally does not understand an event A different from a caused event B. The study of causes is not intended to predict effects, but to explain facts. An Aristotelian cause gives a reason in response to certain why questions. (Aristotle distinguishes four types of causes, which are discussed in more detail here in the Natural Philosophy section).

According to Aristotle, knowledge of causes takes the form of a particular deduction: the demonstration *(apodeixis) of* a syllogism with true premises that state causes for the facts expressed in the conclusion.

Example:

Aristotle speaks of the premises of some demonstrations being principles *(archē;* literally, beginning, origin), first true propositions that cannot themselves be demonstratively proved.

Non-evidentiary sentences

Besides the principles, the existence and the properties of the treated objects of a science as well as certain axioms common to all sciences cannot be proved by demonstrations according to Aristotle, such as the theorem of contradiction. Of the theorem of contradiction Aristotle shows that it cannot be denied. It reads: X cannot occur and not occur to Y at the same time in the same respect (Met. IV 3, 1005b19 f.).

Aristotle argues that whoever denies this must be saying something and thus something definite. If he says e.g. 'man', he designates with it humans and not non-humans.

35

With this determination to something definite, however, he presupposes the theorem of contradiction. This even applies to actions, insofar as a person walks around a well and does not fall into it.

That these propositions and also principles cannot be demonstrated is due to Aristotle's solution of a problem of justification: if knowledge contains justification, then this leads in a concrete case of knowledge either (a) to a regress, (b) to a circle, or (c) to fundamental propositions that cannot be justified. Principles in an Aristotelian demonstrative science are such propositions that are not demonstrated but known in some other way (An. Post. I 3).

The relationship between definition, cause and demonstration

Aristotle also speaks of the fact that, provided the premises are principles, they can also represent definitions. How demonstration, cause and definition relate to each other is illustrated by the following example:The moon exhibits an eclipse at time t because (i) whenever something is in the sun's shadow of the earth, it exhibits an eclipse and (ii) the moon is in the sun's shadow of the earth at time t. *Demonstration:*

Mean term: Occlusion of the sun by the earth. *Cause: Occlusion of the* sun by the earth occurs to the moon at time t.

The definition here would be something like: *Lunar eclipse is the case in which the earth covers the sun.* It does not explain the word 'lunar eclipse'. Rather, it specifies *what* a lunar eclipse is. By stating the cause, one progresses from a fact to its reason. The procedure of analysis is to search bottom-up to a known fact for the next cause until a final cause is reached.

Status of the principles and function of the demonstration

The Aristotelian model of science was understood in modern times and until the 20th century as a top-down method of proof. The unprovable principles were necessarily true and were obtained by induction and intuition *(nous).* All propositions of a science would follow - in an axiomatic structure - from its principles. Accordingly, science is based on two steps: First the principles would be grasped intuitively, then top-down knowledge would be demonstrated from them.

Opponents of this top-down interpretation question, above all, that for Aristotle

1. the principles are always true;

2. the principles are obtained by intuition;

3. the function of demonstration is that knowledge is inferred from supreme principles.

One direction of interpretation claims that the demonstration has a didactic function. Since Aristotle does not follow his theory of science in the scientific writings, the latter do not explain how research should be *carried out,* but how it should be *presented* didactically.

Another interpretation also rejects the didactic interpretation, since applications of the scientific-theoretical model could very well be found in the scientific writings. Above all, however, it criticizes the first reading in that it does not distinguish between knowledge ideal and knowledge culture; for Aristotle considers principles fallible and the function of demonstration heuristic. She reads the demonstration bottom-up: With the help of the demonstration, the causes of known facts are searched for.

The scientific research starts from the empirical (mostly universal) propositions which are more familiar for us. To such a conclusion premises are searched, which indicate causes for the corresponding facts.

The scientific research process consists now, for example, in analyzing the connection of gravity and statue or moon and eclipse in such a way more exactly that one looks for middle terms which connect them as causes with each other. In the simplest case there is only one middle term, in others several.

Top-down, knowledge is then presented from the explanatory premises to the explained universal empirical propositions. In this process, the premises give the reason for the facts described in the conclusion. The goal of any discipline is such a demonstrative presentation of knowledge in which the non-demonstrative principles of that science are premises.

Grasping the principles

How the principles are grasped according to Aristotle remains unclear and is disputed. Presumably, they are formed by general concepts that arise through an inductive process, an ascent within the stages of knowledge described above: Perception becomes memory, repeated perception condenses into experience, and from experience we form general concepts. With this perception-based conception of the formation of general concepts, Aristotle rejects both conceptions that derive general concepts from higher knowledge and those that claim that general concepts are innate. Presumably on the basis of these general concepts the principles, definitions are formed.

The dialectic, which deals with questions in the form 'Is P true of S or not?' is presumably a means of testing principles. The faculty that grasps these basic general concepts and definitions is the mind, insight *(nous)*.

Philosophy of Nature

Nature

In Aristotle's philosophy of nature, nature *(physis)* means two things: On the one hand, the primary subject area consists of things existing by nature (humans, animals, plants, the elements), which are distinct from artifacts. On the other hand, motion *(kínēsis)* and rest *(stasis)* form the origin, respectively the basic principle *(archē)* *of* all nature (Phys. II 1, 192b14).

Movement again means change *(metabolē)* (Phys. II 1,193a30). For example, locomotion is a form of change. Likewise, the "proper movements" of the body as it grows or decreases (for example, through food intake) represent change. Consequently, both concepts, kínēsis and metabolē, are inseparable for Aristotle. Together they form the basic principle and the beginning of all natural things. In the case of artifacts, the principle of all change comes from outside (Phys. II 1, 192b8-22). The science of nature depends in the consequence on the kinds of the change.
"In all things of nature there is something of the marvelous." - Aristoteles

Definition, principles and types of change

A process of change of X is given if X, which (i) according to reality has the property F and (ii) according to possibility has G, realizes the property G. In the case of bronze (X), which is a lump according to reality (F) and a statue according to possibility (G), change is present when the bronze *becomes* the form of a statue according to *reality* (G); the process is complete when the bronze *has* this form. Or if the uneducated Socrates is formed, then a condition is realized, which according to the possibility already existed.

The process of change is thus characterized by its transitional status and presupposes that something that is possible can be realized (Phys. III 1, 201a10-201b5).

For all processes of change, Aristotle (in agreement with his natural philosophical predecessors) considers opposites to be fundamental. He furthermore argues that in a process of change these opposites (like *formed-unformed*) always occur *at* a substrate or underlying *(hypokeimenon)*, so that his model has the following three principles:

1. Substrate of change (X);

2. Initial state of change (F);
3. Target state of change (G).

If the uneducated Socrates is formed, he is thereby at every point of the change Socrates. Accordingly, the bronze remains bronze. The substrate of the change, on which this takes place, remains thereby identical with itself. Aristotle understands the initial state of the change as a state, which lacks the corresponding property of the target state (Privation; Phys. I 7).

Aristotle distinguishes four types of change:

1. Qualitative change

2. Quantitative change

3. Local movement

4. Emergence/Departure.

For every change - according to Aristotle - there is an underlying, numerically identical substrate (Physics I 7, 191a13-15). In the case of qualitative, quantitative and local change this is a concrete single thing which changes its properties, its size or its position. But how does this behave with the emergence/decay of concrete single things?

The Eleatics had put forward the influential thesis that emergence is not possible, because they considered it contradictory, if being emerges from non-being (with emergence from being they saw a similar problem). The solution of the atomists, coming into being is a process, in which by mixing and separation of imperishable and unchangeable atoms new single things emerge from old ones, leads, according to Aristotle's view, coming into being illegitimately back to qualitative change (Gen. Corr. 317a20 ff.).

Form and matter at creation/decay

Aristotle's analysis of coming into being and passing away is based on the innovative distinction between form and matter (hylemorphism). He accepts that no concrete single thing arises from non-being, but analyzes the case of *arising as* follows. A concrete single thing of the type F does not arise from a non-substantial F, but from an underlying substrate which does not have the form F: matter.

A thing is created when matter takes on a new form. Thus, a bronze statue is created by a bronze matter taking on a corresponding form. The finished statue is *made of* bronze, and the bronze underlies the statue as matter. The answer to Eleaten is that to a non-substantial statue corresponds the bronze as matter, which becomes a statue by adding a form. The process of creation is thereby characterized by different degrees of being. The actual, actual, formed statue arises from something that is potentially a statue, namely bronze as matter (Phys. I 8, 191b10-34).

Matter and form are aspects of a concrete single thing and do not appear independently. Matter is always substance of a certain thing, which already has a form. It is a relative abstraction term to form. By structuring such a matter in a new way, a new single thing arises.

A house is composed of form (the blueprint) and matter (wood and bricks). The bricks as matter of the house are by a certain process in a certain way formed, configured clay. By form Aristotle understands more rarely the external shape (this only in the case of artifacts), usually the internal structure or nature, that which is captured by a definition. The form of an object of a certain type describes thereby conditions, which matter is suitable for this and which not.

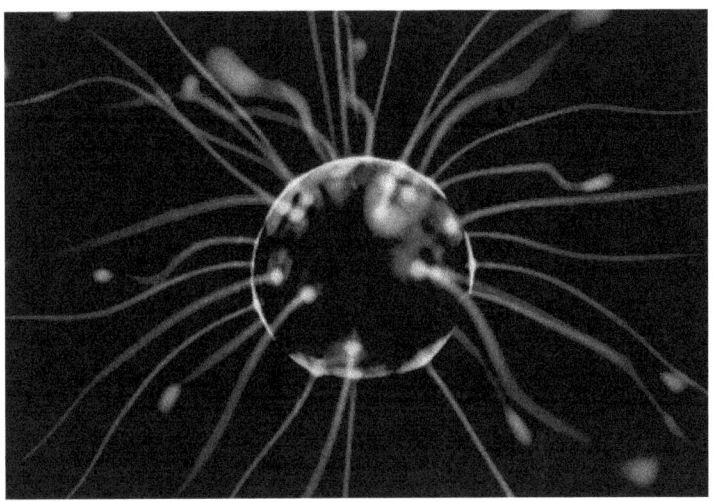

Local movement

According to Aristotle, movements are either natural or unnatural (violent). Only living beings move of their own accord, everything else is either moved by something or it strives as straight as possible towards its natural place and comes to a standstill there.

The natural location of a body depends on the type of matter that predominates in it. When water or earth predominates, the body moves to the center of the earth, the center of the world; when fire or air dominates, it strives upward. Earth is exclusively heavy, fire absolutely light, water relatively heavy, air relatively light. The natural place of fire is above the air and below the lunar sphere.

Lightness and heaviness are properties of bodies which have nothing to do with their density. With the introduction of the idea of an absolute heaviness and absolute lightness (weightlessness of fire), Aristotle rejects the view of Plato and the atomists, who considered all objects to be heavy and understood weight as a relative quantity.

The fifth element, the ether of the sky, is massless and moves eternally in uniform circular motion around the center of the world. The ether fills the space above the lunar sphere; it is not subject to any change except the local movement. The assumption that on the earth and in the sky different laws are valid is necessary for Aristotle, because the movement of the planets and fixed stars does not come to rest.

Aristotle assumes that for every local motion a medium, which either acts as a moving force or resists the motion, is necessary; a continuous motion in a vacuum is impossible in principle. Aristotle even excludes the existence of a vacuum.

Aristotle's theory of motion was influential until Galileo and Newton developed a new concept of inertia.

Causes

According to Aristotle, in order to have knowledge of processes of change and thus of nature, one must know the corresponding causes *(aitiai)* (Phys. I 1, 184a10-14). Aristotle claims that there are exactly four types of causes, each of which answers the question *why in* a different way and which, as a rule, must all be stated in a complete explanation (Phys. II 3, 194b23-35):

The Aristotelian concept of cause differs to a large extent from the modern one. As a rule, for the explanation of the same state of affairs or object, different causes apply at the same time. The cause of form often coincides with the cause of motion and the final cause. Thus, the cause of a house is brick and wood, the building plan, the architect and the protection against bad weather. The latter three often coincide, insofar as, for example, the purpose of *protection against bad weather* determines the building plan (in the mind) of the architect.

The final cause has been criticized from the point of view of modern mechanistic physics. However, Aristotle largely sets himself apart from an altogether teleologically oriented nature as in Plato. For him, final causes occur in nature mainly in biology, namely in the functional structure of living beings and the reproduction of species.

Metaphysics

"Metaphysics involves intuitive knowledge of unprovable starting-points concepts and truth and demonstrative knowledge of what follows from them." - Aristoteles

Metaphysics as First Philosophy

Aristotle does not use the term "metaphysics". Nevertheless, one of his most important works traditionally bears this title. The *Metaphysics* is a collection of individual investigations compiled by a later editor, covering a more or less coherent range of topics by asking about the principles and causes of being and about the science responsible for them. Whether the title (*ta meta ta physika:* the <writings, things> according to physics) has a merely bibliographical or a factual background is unclear.

In the *Metaphysics,* Aristotle speaks of a science superior to all other sciences, which he calls First Philosophy, wisdom *(sophia),* or theology. This First Philosophy is characterized in this collection of individual investigations in three ways:

1. as a science of the most general principles central to Aristotle's philosophy of science (→ Theorem of Contradiction).

2. as science of being as being, the Aristotelian ontology

3. as a science of the divine, Aristotelian theology (→ theology).

Whether or to what extent these three projects are interrelated aspects of the same science or independent individual projects is controversial. Aristotle treats later metaphysically named topics also in other writings.

Ontology

In the Corpus Aristotelicum, different theories of being are found in two works, the early *Categories* and the late *Metaphysics.*

Substances in the categories

The *Categories, which* form the first writing in the *Organon,* are probably the most influential work of Aristotle and of the history of philosophy in general.

The early ontology of *categories* deals with the questions 'What is that which actually exists?' and 'How is that which exists ordered?' and is to be understood as a criticism of Plato's position. The presumed train of thought can be sketched as follows. Properties are distinguished, which are assigned to single things (P is assigned to S). There are two possible interpretations: the actual being, the substance *(ousia)* are

1. abstract, independently existing archetypes as cause and object of cognition of properties.

2. concrete individual things as carriers of properties.

Aristotle himself reports (Met. I 6) that Plato taught that one must distinguish from the perceptible single things separate, not sensually perceptible, unchangeable, eternal archetypes. Plato assumed that there cannot be definitions (and thus from his point of view also knowledge) of the single things which change constantly.

For him, the object of definition and knowledge are the archetypes (ideas) as that which is causative for the order structure of being. This can be clarified by a single and numerically identical idea of man, which is separate from all men, which is causal for the respective being of man and which is the object of knowledge for the question 'What is a man?

Aristotle's division of being into *categories* seems to differ from Plato's outlined position. He is oriented to the linguistic structure of simple sentences of the form 'S is P' and the linguistic practice, whereby he does not explicitly separate the linguistic and the ontological level.

Some expressions - like 'Socrates' - can only occupy the subject position S in this linguistic structure, everything else is predicated of them. The things that fall into this category of substance, which he calls *First Substance,* are ontologically independent; they do not require any other thing to exist. Therefore, they are ontologically primary, for everything else depends on them and nothing would exist without them.

These dependent properties require a single thing, a first substance as a carrier, *at* which they occur. Such properties (e.g. white, sitting) can belong to a single thing (e.g. Socrates) or not and are therefore accidental properties. This concerns everything outside the category of the substance.

For some properties (e.g. 'human being') it is now valid that they can be stated in such a way by a single thing (e.g. Socrates) that their definition (reasonable living being) is also valid by this single thing. Therefore, they *necessarily* come to him. These are the species and the genus. Because of this close relation, in which the species and the genus indicate *what* a first substance is respectively (for instance in the answer to the question 'What is Socrates?': 'a human being'), Aristotle calls it second substance. Thereby also a second substance depends ontologically on a first substance.

- A) Category of the substance:

    o 1. substance: characteristic of independence.

    o 2. substance: characteristic of recognizability.

- B) Non-substantial categories: Accidentals.

Aristotle thus argues the following theses:

1. Only single things (first substances) are independent and therefore ontologically primary.

2. All properties depend on the individual things. There are no independent, non-exemplified archetypes.

3. Besides contingent, accidental properties (like 'white') there are necessary, essential properties (like 'human'), which indicate what a single thing is in each case.

The substance theory of metaphysics

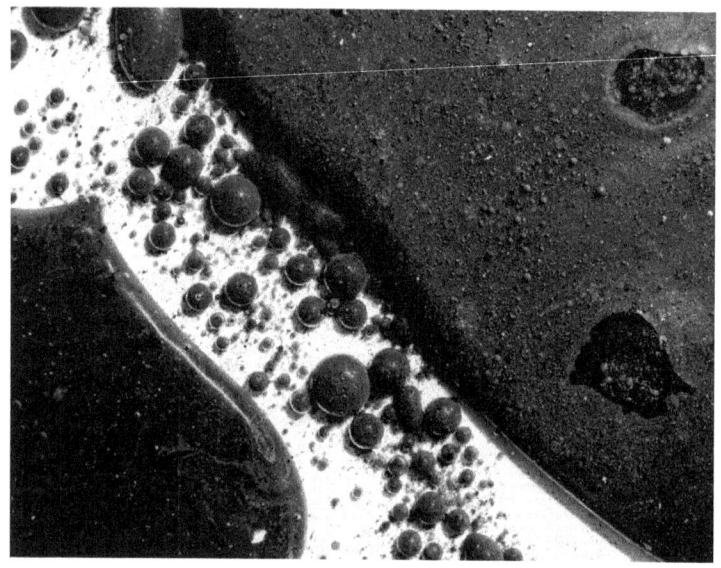

For Plato, the consequence of his conception of the ideas is the assumption that in the proper, independent sense only the unchanging ideas exist; the individual things exist only in dependence on the ideas. Aristotle criticizes this ontological consequence in detail in the *Metaphysics*. He considers it contradictory that the adherents of the doctrine of ideas on the one hand distinguish the ideas from the sense objects by assigning them the characteristic of generality and thus undifferentiatedness, and on the other hand at the same time assume a separate existence for each individual idea; thereby the ideas themselves would become individual things, which is incompatible with their defining characteristic of generality (Met. XIII 9, 1086a32-34).

In the *Metaphysics,* Aristotle, as part of his project to investigate being as being, argues that all being is either a substance or is related to one (*Metaphysics* IV 2).

In the *categories* he had formulated a criterion for substances and had given examples (Socrates) for them. In the *Metaphysics,* he now thematizes the substance again, in order to search for the principles and causes of a substance, of a concrete single thing. Here he now asks: What makes for instance Socrates a substance? Substance here is thus a two-digit predicate *(substance of X), so* that one can formulate the question thus: *What is the substance-X of a substance?* Here the form-matter distinction, which is not present in the *categories,* plays a crucial role.

Aristotle seems to search for the substance-X primarily by means of two criteria, which are distributed between the first and the second substance in the theory of *categories:*

- (i) independent existence or subject for everything else, but not being predicate itself (individual being = first substance);

- (ii) To be an object of definition, to guarantee cognizability, that is, to answer the question 'What is X?' (general essence = second substance).

The criterion (ii) is more precisely fulfilled by Aristotle's definition of essence as substance-X. By essence he means here what corresponds ontologically to a definition

(Met. VII 4; 5, 1031a12; VIII 1, 1042a17). Essence describes the necessary properties without which a single thing would cease to be one and the same thing. Ask: *What is the cause of this portion of matter being Socrates?*, Aristotle's answer is: *the essence of Socrates, which is neither another constituent* apart from *the material constituents* (in which case it would require another structural principle to explain how it is united with the material constituents) *nor something* composed of *material constituents* (in which case it would be necessary to explain how the essence itself is composed).

Aristotle identifies the form *(eidos)* of a single thing as its essence and thus as substance-X. By form he means not so much the outer shape as the structure: The form

- is inherent in the individual thing,

- causes

    ○ in the case of living beings, the emergence of a specimen of the same species (Met. VII 8, 1033b30-2)

    ○ in the case of artifacts (e.g. house) as formal cause (blueprint) (Met. VII 9, 1034a24) in the mind of the producer (Met. VII 7, 1032b23) (architect) the origin of the single thing.

- precedes the emergence of a single thing composed of form and matter and does not emerge and change, thus causing (in natural species) a continuity of forms that is eternal for Aristotle (Met. VII 8, 1033b18)

- is cause, explanation of the essential properties and faculties of an individual thing (for example, the form of a human being is the soul (Met. VII 10, 1035b15), which is constituted by faculties such as nutritive faculty, perceptive faculty, reasoning faculty, among others (An. II 2, 413b11-13)).

That the form as substance-X must also fulfill the mentioned criterion (ii) of being independent, and this is partly taken as a criterion for something individual, is one of many aspects in the following central interpretational controversy: Does Aristotle conceive of form (A) as something general or (B) as something individual (to the respective individual thing)?

Formulated as a problem: How can the form, the *eidos, be* at the same time form of a single thing and object of knowledge? For (A) speaks in particular that Aristotle assumes in several places that the substance-X and thus the form is definable (Met. VII 13) and this applies for him (as for Plato) only to general things (VII 11, 1036a; VII 15, 1039b31-1040a2). For (B), on the other hand, speaks above all that Aristotle seems to represent categorically the un-Platonic position: No general can be substance-X (Met. VII 13).

According to (B) Socrates and Callias possess two also qualitatively different forms. Definable then would have to be separable, supra-individual aspects of these two forms. The interpretation (A), on the other hand, solves the dilemma, for instance, by interpreting the statement *Kein Allgemeines ist Substanz-X* as *Nichts allgemein Prädizierbares ist Substanz-X* and thus defusing it. The form is not predicated in the conventional way (like the kind 'man' of 'Socrates' in the *Categories*) and is therefore not general in the problematic sense. Rather, the form is 'predicated' by the indeterminate matter in a way that first constitutes an individual object.

Nude and potency

"The energy of the mind is the essence of life." - Aristoteles

The relationship between form and matter, which is important for ontology, is explained in more detail by another pair of terms: act *(energeia, entelecheia)* and potency *(dynamis)*.

For the form-matter distinction the later ontologically named meaning of potency or capability is important.Potentiality is here a state, which is opposed by another state - actuality - in that an object is according to reality F or according to capability, according to possibility. Thus a boy is a man according to possibility, an uneducated man is an educated one according to possibility (Met. IX 6).

This relation of actuality and potentiality (described here diachronically) forms the basis for the relation of form and matter (which is also to be understood synchronously), because form and matter are aspects of a single thing, not its parts. They are connected with each other in the relation of actuality and potentiality and thus (only) constitute the single thing.

Accordingly, the matter of a single thing is *potentially* exactly what the form of the single thing and the single thing itself are *actual* (Met. VIII 1, 1042a27 f.; VIII 6, 1045a23-33; b17-19). On the one hand, it is true (viewed diachronically) that a particular portion of bronze is potentially a sphere as well as a statue. But on the other hand (synchronically as a constituent aspect) the bronze on a statue is potentially exactly what the statue and its form are actual. The bronze of the statue is a constituent of the statue, but is not identical with it.

And so flesh and bones are also potentially what Socrates or his form (the configuration and capabilities of his material components typical of a human being,→ psychology) are actual.

Just as form is primary to matter, actuality is primary to potentiality for Aristotle (Met. IX 8, 1049b4-5). Among other things, it is primary to cognition. One can only state a faculty by reference to the actuality to which it is a faculty. The faculty of seeing, for instance, can only be specified by referring to the activity 'seeing' (Met. IX 8, 1049b12-17). Furthermore, actuality is also temporally earlier than potentiality in the crucial sense, because a human being comes into being through a human being who is actual human being (Met. IX 8, 1049b17-27).

Theology

Aristotle distinguishes three possible substances in the run-up to his theology: (i) sensuously perceptible perishable, (ii) sensuously perceptible eternal, and (iii) non-sensuously perceptible eternal and immutable (Met. XII 1, 1069a30-1069b2). (i) are the concrete single things (of the sublunar sphere), (ii) the eternal, moved celestial bodies, (iii) proves to be the itself unmoved origin of all movement.

Aristotle argues for a divine mover by stating that if all substances were transient, everything would have to be transient, but time and change themselves are necessarily imperishable (Phys. VIII 1, 251a8-252b6; Met. XII 6, 1071b6-10).

According to Aristotle, the only change which can exist eternally is the circular motion (Phys. VIII 8-10; Met. XII 6,1071b11). The corresponding observable circular motion of the fixed stars must therefore have as cause an eternal and immaterial substance (Met. XII 8, 1073b17-32). If the essence of this substance contained potentiality, the movement could be interrupted. Therefore it must be pure actuality, activity (Met. XII, 1071b12-22). As the last principle, this mover itself must be unmoved.

According to Aristotle, the unmoved mover moves "like a beloved," namely as a goal (Met. XII 7, 1072b3), because the desired, the thought, and especially the beloved can move without being moved (Met. XII 7, 1072a26). Its activity is the most pleasurable and beautiful. Since it is immaterial reason *(nous)* and its activity consists in thinking the best object, it thinks itself: the "thinking of thinking" *(noêsis noêseôs)* (Met. XII 9, 1074b34 f.). Moreover, since only living things can think, he must be alive. Aristotle identifies the motionless mover with God (Met. XII 7, 1072b23 ff.).

The unmoved mover moves the whole nature. The fixed star sphere moves, because it imitates the perfection with the circular movement. The other heavenly bodies are moved mediated by the fixed star sphere. The living beings have a share in eternity, in that they exist eternally by means of reproduction (GA II 1, 731b31-732a1).

Biology

Position of biology

Aristotle occupies an important place not only in the history of philosophy, but also in the history of the natural sciences. A large part of his surviving writings is natural scientific, of which by far the most important and extensive are the biological writings, which comprise almost a third of the surviving body of work. Presumably in division of labor, botany was edited by his closest collaborator Theophrastus, medicine by his student Menon.

Aristotle compares the study of imperishable substances (God and celestial bodies) and imperishable substances (the living beings). Both fields of research have their attraction. The imperishable substances, the highest objects of knowledge, give the greatest pleasure to study, but the knowledge of living beings is easier to obtain, because they are closer to us.

He emphasizes the value of studying even lower animals, pointing out that they, too, show something natural and beautiful that is not exhausted in their disassembled components, but emerges only through the activities and interaction of the parts (PA I 5, 645a21-645b1).

"If one way be better than another, that you may be sure is nature's way. " - Aristoteles

Aristotle as an empirical researcher

Aristotle himself did empirical research, but probably not experiments in the sense of a methodical experimental set-up - introduced only in modern natural science.

It is certain that he performed dissections himself. The closest thing to an experiment is the examination of fertilized hen's eggs, repeated at fixed intervals, with the aim of observing the order in which the organs develop (GA VI 3, 561a6-562a20).

However, experiments are not the essential instrument of research in his actual domain - descriptive zoology - either. In addition to his own observations and a few text sources, he also relied here on information from relevant professionals such as fishermen, beekeepers, hunters and shepherds. He had the contents of his text sources partially empirically verified, but also uncritically adopted foreign errors. One lost work probably consisted largely of drawings and diagrams of animals.

Methodology of biology: separation of facts and causes

Because of the long-prevailing interpretive model of Aristotle's philosophy of science and the neglect of his biological writings, it was once assumed that he did not apply this theory to biology. In contrast, it is now well accepted that his approach to biology was influenced by his philosophy of science, although the extent and degree are disputed.

Fact Collections

No description of Aristotle's scientific approach has survived. Preserved, besides the general theory of science, are only texts that represent a final product of scientific research. The biological writings are arranged in a certain order, which corresponds to the procedure.

The first writing *(Historia animalium)* describes the different animal species and their specific differences. It offers the collection of the factual material such as that all living beings with lungs have windpipes. It does not discuss whether something is necessary or impossible to be so. In the collection of facts, Aristotle arranges living things according to various classification characteristics such as blood-bearing, viviparous, etc. Arranged according to characteristics, he establishes general relations between different aspects of the constitution.

For example, he remarks: All quadrupeds that are viviparous have lungs and tracheae (HA II 15, 505b32 f.). Only the writings *De generatione animalium* (On the Origin of Animals) and *De partibus animalium* (On the Parts of Animals), which follow and build on this work, deal with the causes that explain the facts.

Cause knowledge

The collection of facts is the prerequisite for achieving knowledge based on knowledge of causes. Central to biology are final causes, which indicate the purpose of the components of the body. For Aristotle, the cause of the existence of a trachea in all living beings that possess a lung is the functioning of the lung.

The lungs, unlike the stomach, cannot connect directly to the mouth because they require a bifurcated channel so that inhalation and exhalation are possible in an optimal way. Since this channel must be of a certain length, all creatures with lungs have a throat. Fish, therefore, do not have a throat because they do not need a trachea, since they breathe with gills (PA III 3, 664a14-34).

Final causes in biology

The use of final explanations in biology (and also other fields of Aristotle's research) has been widely criticized, especially in the early modern period and into the 20th century. By final explanations or causes Aristotle understands here, however, as a rule, no overarching purposes, which would have, for example, a particular species. He is rather concerned with an internal determination of the function of organisms and their parts.

Zoology contents

Aristotle studied over 500 species. His writings systematically discuss the internal and external parts of each animal, components such as blood and bones, modes of reproduction, food, habitat, and behavior. He describes the behavior of domestic animals, exotic predators such as the crocodile, birds, insects, and marine animals. For this purpose, he orders the living creatures.

Classification of species

Aristotle distinguishes two main groups of living beings: blood-bearing and bloodless animals. This corresponds to the division into vertebrates and invertebrates. He arranges these according to largest genera:

- Blood-bearing animals:

    o viviparous quadrupeds

    o egg-laying quadrupeds

    o Birds

- Fish

- Cetaceans (marine mammals)

- oviparous footless (snakes)

- viviparous footless (vipers)

- Man (forms an isolated genus)

- Bloodless animals:

  - Molluscs

  - Crustaceans

  - Shuttering animals

  - Notch animals

Probably it was not Aristotle's intention to create a complete taxonomy. The system of a taxonomy is also no main object for him. The aim of his investigations was rather a morphology, a classification of the living beings on the basis of characteristic features. Thus he did not fix terminologically the genera between the mentioned as well as subgenera.

Fact: Aristotle is the founder of zoology: Aristotle was a man ahead of his time. He had new ideas on how to study the world. He used to make detailed observations of the world and recorded what he saw. In his quest to learn more about the anatomy of animals he started dissecting them, which was a new practice. Greek philosophers and educators of those times used to do all their work in their mind, thinking about the world without observing it.

Example of description. The octopus

Aristotle and the findings of modern biology

In many cases Aristotle was mistaken as a biologist. Some of his errors seem quite curious, such as the description of the bison that "defends itself by lashing out and expelling its excrement, which it can fling as far as seven and a half meters from itself" (HA IX 45, 630b8 f.). Apparently, his source of information about this exotic animal was not very reliable.

Other well-known misconceptions include the claim that the male has more teeth than the female (HA II 3, 501b19), that the brain is a cooling organ, and that thinking occurs in the heart region (PA II 7, 652b21-25; III 3, 514a16-22), and the concept of telegony, according to which a previous pregnancy may influence the phenotype of offspring from subsequent pregnancies.

However, Aristotle also gained insights based on his observations that are not only true, but have been rediscovered or confirmed only in modern times. For example, in describing the octopus cited, he mentions that mating occurs through a tentacle of the male that is forked - so-called hectocotylization - and describes this reproductive process (HA V 5, 541b9-15; V 12, 544a12;

GA V 15, 720b33). This phenomenon was known only through Aristotle until the 19th century; the exact nature of reproduction was not fully verified until 1959.

Even more significant is his hypothesis according to which the parts of an organism are formed in a hierarchical order and are not - as the preformation theory (already advocated by Anaxagoras) assumes - preformed (GA 734a28-35). This view of embryonic development has become known in modern times under the name epigenesis, which was not yet used by Aristotle. Its empirical basis for Aristotle were his dissections.

In modern times, however, the preformation theory was the generally accepted theory from the 17th to the 19th century, and representatives of epigenesis such as William Harvey (1651) and Caspar Friedrich Wolff (1759) attracted little attention with their embryological studies, which clearly showed that embryos develop from entirely undifferentiated matter. This insight prevailed only in the early 19th century and eventually supplanted the preformist speculations.

It was finally confirmed only in the 20th century in experimental biology by Hans Driesch and Hans Spemann that embryonic development is a chain of new formations, an epigenetic process. Furthermore, there is an analogy between Aristotelian goal-directed epigenesis and genetics.

Theory of the soul: theory of being alive

Initial situation

Living beings differ from other natural and artificial objects in that they are alive. In Homer, the soul *(psychê)* is that which leaves a corpse. In the course of the 6th and 5th centuries B.C., the concept increasingly finds a significant expansion: to be animate *(empsychos)* means to be alive, and the concept soul now also has cognitive and emotional aspects. Aristotle takes up this use of language.

In his theory of the soul he is confronted with two positions: on the one hand with the materialism of pre-Socratic natural philosophers (especially Democritus and Empedocles), who claim that the soul consists of a special

66

kind of matter, on the other hand with the dualistic position of Plato, for whom the soul is immortal, immaterial and according to its nature rather something intelligible.

Regarding the dispute between materialism and dualism, whether body and soul are identical with each other or not, Aristotle is of the opinion that the question is wrongly posed. He explains this with a comparison: The question *Are body and soul identical?* is as nonsensical as the question *Are wax and its form identical?* (An. II 1, 412b6-9). States of the soul are always also states of the body, but Aristotle denies an identity of body and soul as well as the immortality of the soul.

Destination of the soul

What the soul is, Aristotle determines by means of his distinction of form and matter. The soul relates to the body like the form to the matter, that is like a statue form to the bronze. However, form and matter of a single thing are not two different *objects,* not its parts, but aspects of this very single thing.

Aristotle defines the soul as the "first actuality *(entelecheia)* of a natural organic body" (An. II 1, 412b5 f.). A reality or actuality is the soul, because it represents as form the aspect of the living at the potentially animated matter (namely the organic). It is a *first actuality* insofar as the living being is alive even when it is only asleep and does not perform any other activities (which are also aspects of the soulful). (An. II 1, 412a19-27).

Skills

The further mental aspects are the functions that are characteristic for a living being, its specific abilities or capacities *(dynamis)*. Aristotle distinguishes above all the following abilities:

- Nutritional and reproductive capacity *(threptikon)*

- Perception *(aisthêtikon)*

- Thinking *(dianoêtikon)*

Nourishing and reproductive ability - as a fundamental ability of all living things - also come to the plants, perceptive ability (and locomotion ability) show only the animals (including the human being). The thinking possesses alone the human being.

Perception

"The aim of art is to represent not the outward appearance of things, but their inward significance." - Aristoteles

Aristotle distinguishes the following five senses and claims that there cannot be more:

1. Sense of touch

2. Sense of taste

3. Smell

4. Listen

5. View

Perception *(aisthesis) is* generally understood by Aristotle as a suffering or a qualitative change (An. II 5, 416b33 f.). What the senses perceive is determined by a continuous pair of opposites: seeing by light and dark, hearing by high and low, smelling and tasting by bitter and sweet; touching has different pairs of opposites: hard and soft, hot and cold, wet and dry.

Aristotle claims that in the process of perception the respective organ becomes *like the* thing perceived (An. 418a3-6). Furthermore, he says that the organ takes in the form "without the matter," just as "the wax takes in the seal of the ring without iron and without gold" (An. II 12, 424a18 f.). This has been interpreted by some commentators, including Thomas Aquinas, to mean that the organ does not undergo a natural change *(mutatio naturalis)* but a spiritual one *(mutatio spiritualis).* Other interpreters think that "without matter" simply means that no particles enter the organ, but it actually changes according to the object of perception.

The sense of touch possesses all living beings, which possess perception. The sense of touch is a sense of contact, that is, there is no medium between the organ of perception and the thing perceived (An. II 11, 423a13 f.). The sense of taste is a kind of sense of touch (An. II 10, 422a8 f.). The three distance senses of smell, hearing and sight, on the other hand, require a medium that transports the impression from the perceived to the organ.

Reason

Reason or the faculty of thought *(nous)* is specific to man. Aristotle defines it as "that by which the soul thinks and makes assumptions" (An. III 4, 429a22 f.). Reason is incorporeal, since otherwise it would be limited in its possible objects of thought, which may not be the case (An. III 4, 429a17-22). However, it is bodily bound, since it depends on conceptions *(phantasmata).* Ideas form the material of the acts of thinking; they are conserved sense perceptions.

The corresponding imaginative faculty (*phantasia;* neither interpretive nor productive in the sense of fantasy) is dependent on sense impressions, although sense impression and imagination can sometimes differ greatly in quality, for example in hallucinations. Imagination is assigned to the perceptual faculties (An. III 8, 428b10-18). Insofar as reason is bound to ideas in its activity, it is also bound to a body.

Ethics

Happiness *(eudaimonia)* and virtue or best state *(aretê)* are the central concepts in Aristotle's ethics. Aristotle argues that the goal of all intentional actions is happiness realized in the "good life." In his view, the formation of virtues is essential for achieving this goal (→ virtue ethics).

Happiness as the goal of the good life

Hierarchy of aspirations of goods

In their (intentional) actions, all people strive for something that seems good to them. Some of these aspired goods are aspired to only as a means to achieve other goods, others are both a means and a good themselves. Since striving cannot be infinite, there must be a supreme good and ultimate goal of striving. This is pursued only for its own sake. It is apparently commonly called "happiness" *(eudaimonia)* (EN I 1).

Definition of happiness as the supreme good

In order to outline what happiness consists of as the supreme good for man, Aristotle asks: What is the specific function *(telos)* or task *(ergon)* of man? It consists in the faculty of reason *(logos), which* distinguishes him from other living beings. The part of the soul that is specific to man has this faculty of reason; the other part of the soul, which is composed of emotions and desires, is not itself rational, but it can be guided by reason.

In order to attain happiness, the individual must use the faculty of reason, not merely possess it, in perpetuity and in a best state *(aretê).* Accordingly, "the good for man", happiness, is a

Virtues

In order to attain the state of excellence, one must form (a) virtues of mind and (b) virtues of character according to the two parts of the soul. For Aristotle, virtues are attitudes to which every human being has the disposition, but which must first be formed through education and habituation.

71

Mind Virtues

Among the mind virtues, some relate to the knowledge of immutables or the production of objects. Prudence *(phronêsis)* alone is related to action, as a virtue with the goal of a good life. It is necessary - along with the virtues of character - to be able to act in concrete decision-making situations with regard to the good life. In the realm of human actions, unlike in the sciences, there is no proof, and to be wise in this regard also requires experience. The function of prudence is to choose the middle *(mesotês)*.

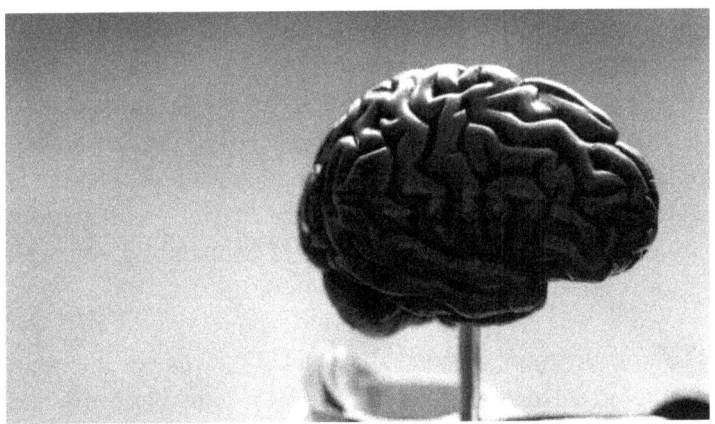

Character Virtues

Character virtues are attitudes *(hexeis)* for which it is characteristic that they can be praised and blamed. They are formed by education and habituation, although this is not to be understood as conditioning. Although a great deal depends on habituation from childhood (EN II 1, 1103b24), character virtues are not present until someone knowingly chooses the appropriate actions, not because of possible sanctions, but for the sake of the virtuous actions themselves, and when he does not waver in doing so (EN II 3, 1105a26-33).

Also, the virtuous person differs from the self-controlled person (who may perform the same actions but must force himself to do so) in that he takes pleasure in virtue (EN II 2, 1104b3 ff.).

By habituation, the virtues of character are pronounced by avoiding excess and deficiency.

The instrument of the middle determines the character virtues more precisely. For example, the virtue of bravery is a middle between the vices of foolhardiness and cowardice. The basis for the virtues are the actions as well as the emotions and desires. Not brave but foolhardy is someone who is either completely fearless in a certain situation, although the situation is threatening, or who ignores his fear in a serious threatening situation.

The middle, then, consists - here as in the case of the other character virtues - in having appropriate emotions and acting accordingly. At the same time, this doctrine of the middle is presumably not to be understood as normatively guiding action in concrete situations, but only as a descriptive instrument of the virtues of character. It is also *not an arithmetical* middle, but a middle *for us (pros hêmas),* which takes into account the respective emotion, the person as well as the situation.

Life forms and desire

In the context of the analysis of the good life, Aristotle distinguishes three forms of life that pursue different goals:

1. the pleasure life - with the goal of pleasure;

2. political life - with the goal of honor;

3. the theoretical life - with the goal of knowledge (EN I 3).

Aristotle considers the life of pleasure in the sense of a mere satisfaction of desires to be slavish and rejects it. He does not consider the acquisition of money and wealth as a goal to be a form of life, since money is always only a means to an end, but never an end itself. He pleads for the theoretical life as the best form of life.

The best activity sought in the definition of happiness is that of the theorist who researches and gains new knowledge in such fields as philosophy, mathematics, etc., for it means leisure, serves no other purpose, actuates the best in man with the virtues of understanding, and exhibits the best objects of knowledge (EN X 7, 1177a18-35).

Although he considers theoretical life to be the best possible, he points out that contemplation as a form of life transcends man as man and is rather something divine (EN X 7, 1177b26-31).

The second best life is the political one. It consists in the exercise of the virtues of character, which govern our dealings with other people as well as with our emotions.

Since virtues of character and virtues of intellect are not mutually exclusive, Aristotle may mean that even the theorist, insofar as he is a social being endowed with emotions, has to operate in terms of the second-best life.

Aristotle considers the activity of the intellectual virtues (at least prudence) and the virtues of character as essential elements of happiness. But he also considers external or physical goods and also pleasure as conditions that are helpful or even necessary to become happy. Goods such as wealth, friends and power we use as means. If some goods are missing, happiness is clouded, as in the case of physical deformity, loneliness, or wayward children (EN I 9, 1099a31-1099b6).

Aristotle thinks that the life of pleasure does not lead to happiness. He does not consider pleasure to be the supreme good. However, in the face of positions hostile to pleasure, he argues that the good life must include pleasure and refers to pleasure as a good (EN VII 14). He also thinks that a virtuous person who is "braided on the wheel" cannot be called happy (EN VII 14, 1153b18-20).

Against Plato's view that pleasures are processes *(kinêsis) that* remove a deficiency (like pleasure in quenching thirst), and thus the completion of the process is better than the process itself, Aristotle argues that pleasures are activities *(energeia) that have* no goal apart from themselves. Paradigmatic cases are perceiving and thinking.

With this concept of pleasure, which defines pleasure as "unimpeded activity" or "perfection of activity" (EN VII 13, 1153a14 f.; X 4, 1174b33), he asserts that the activity of the mind virtues and the character virtues can be pleasurable. Whether pleasures are good or bad depends on whether the corresponding activities are good or bad. In the case of bodily pleasures, the latter is the case, for example, if they occur in excess or if they prevent good actions and are thus detrimental to happiness.

"Happiness is the meaning and the purpose of life, the whole aim and end of human existence." - Aristoteles

Political philosophy

Aristotle's political philosophy follows on from his ethics. As a comprehensive form of all communities, the state *(polis)* exists for the sake of the highest good, happiness (EN I 1, 1094a26-b11; Pol. I 1, 1252a1-7). Thus, political philosophy asks about the conditions of happiness with regard to life in the state. For this purpose, it analyzes the components of every human community and of every state and examines which constitution *(politeia) is the* best and for which particular conditions which constitution is the right one.

Origin, components and purpose of the state

From Aristotle's point of view, the state exists by nature because the individual human being is not able to exist on his own. Looking at the parts of the state composed of the individual households, there are first of all two basic relationships: that between man and woman, whose purpose is procreation, and that of master and slave, which serves subsistence and the increase of property. (Pol. I 2, 1253b, 1253a and 1253b)

Aristotle justifies slavery by conceiving it as conforming to the principle of domination and subordination. He argues that there are slaves who are by nature destined for nothing other than being slaves. He justifies this by arguing that such "slaves by nature" have only a small share in reason; therefore, it is not only justified but even advantageous for themselves that they must spend their lives as slaves (Pol. I 5, 1254b20-23; 1255a1 f.).

However, his concept is unclear and contradictory, since he approves the manumission of slaves in principle and does not give clear criteria for the distinction between accidental slaves (e.g. through captivity in war) and slaves by nature. His advice to promise freedom to slaves as a reward (Pol. VII 10, 1330a20 f.) contradicts the idea of a "slave by nature."

Accordingly, he also argues for the subordination of women (Pol. VII 10, 1330a20 f.). It is better for her to be dominated by the man, since her power of judgment is weaker than that of the man (Pol. I 5, 1254b10-15; I 13, 1259a12).

Several households make up a village in which the division of labor makes better provision possible, and several villages make up a state. This is self-sufficient in the sense that it can provide the conditions for a good life. Aristotle distinguishes the reason for the emergence of the state from its purpose. The state arises for the purpose of survival, of life itself, but its purpose is the *good* life: εὖ ζῆν = eu zēn = living well (Pol. I 2, 1252a25-1253a1).

According to Aristotle, it is part of man's nature to live in community, for he is a "zôon politikon," a living being in the polis community (Pol. I 2, 1253a3). Only in the state can man realize the good life. Whoever does not need the state is "either an animal or a god" (Pol. I 2, 1253a29).

Citizens and constitution of a state

A polis (a state) consists of the free citizens. The purpose of the state is always the good life. Military or trade alliances, i.e. treaties, do not constitute a state. The distinguishing feature of a particular state is its constitution.

The citizen

Citizens are those inhabitants endowed with civil rights who actively participate in the political process (in judging and governing) (Pol. III 1, 1275a22). Aristotle thus defines the citizen primarily not by origin or place of residence, but by participation in the political institutions of the state.

In accordance with the conditions in Athens at the time, Aristotle does not consider women, children, slaves, and strangers to be citizens. A citizen must also not have to work for a living. Thus, wage laborers and craftsmen cannot be citizens (Pol. III 5, 1278a11). The respective constitution of a state determines more precisely who is a citizen and who is not.

Theory of constitutions

In his distinction of the different constitutions, Aristotle asks two questions:

1. Who rules?

2. For whose benefit is it ruled?

For the first question, he distinguishes three possible answers: one, few, many. For the second question, he distinguishes two possible states and beneficiaries: the constitution is just when governing for the benefit of all; it is unjust or misguided when governing solely for the benefit of the rulers (Pol. III 6, 1279a17-21).

On this basis, he drafts a first theory of state forms with six constitutions (Pol, III 6-8):

Different constitutions apply distributive justice in different ways (Pol. III 9, 1280a7-22). He defines distributive justice as distribution proportional to merit or dignity (EN V 6).

Criticism of bad constitutions

Among bad constitutions that are not oriented toward the common good, he considers tyranny the worst, because in it the tyrant rules over the state in the sense of despotic autocracy, like the master over the slave (Pol. III 8, 1279b16).

He considers the oligarchy, which is characterized by the rule of the rich, to be somewhat less bad, as it is very unstable, just like tyranny (Pol. V 12). Aristotle considers the basic error of oligarchy to be the view that those who are unequal in *one* respect (property) are unequal in *all* respects. Similarly, the fundamental error of democracy is the view that those who are equal in *some respects* are equal in *all* respects (Pol. V 1, 1301a25-36).

Aristotle considers democracy to be less bad than tyranny and oligarchy. Besides equality, it is characterized by freedom. Freedom means to live as one wants, equality that governing and being governed goes around (1317b2-12). Aristotle considers absolute freedom to live as one wishes problematic in that it conflicts with the rule of the constitution (Pol. V 9, 1310a30-35).

He criticizes equality when it is interpreted as a total arithmetic, which leads to the fact that the rule of the unwealthy dispossesses the wealthy. Aristotle's so-called "summation thesis" (Pol. III 11, 1281 a38-b9) and his differentiated examination of the forms of popular rule in the context of his second theory of forms of state further indicate that he did not reject the participation of the "common people" in rule outright.

Good constitutions

Among the good constitutions, monarchy (by which Aristotle understands not necessarily a kingship, but only an autocracy serving the common good) is the least good. Insofar as it is not bound by law, it is a mere form of rule, in part hardly a constitution, and problematic insofar as only the law can rule uninfluenced by emotions.

By an aristocracy he understands a rule of the good, that is, of those who have the most share in virtue *(aretê)*, which does not necessarily mean rule by a natal nobility. Since the goal of the state, the good life, is realized to the highest degree in an aristocracy, Aristotle considers it (along with a certain form of monarchy, namely kingship) to be the best constitution (Pol. IV 2, 1289a30-32).
However, Aristotle does not discuss constitutional theory without reference to reality. Often, in his view, an absolute best constitution is not possible in a given state. What is best for a concrete state must always be determined relative to the circumstances (Pol. IV 1, 1288b21-33).

Such considerations pervade the entire constitutional theory. They are particularly evident in the model of politie that Aristotle considers the best possible for most contemporary states (Pol. IV 11, 1295a25). It is a mixed constitution, containing elements of democracy and

oligarchy. It balances the aspirations for equality on the one hand and for wealth on the other.
This balance is achieved, among other things, by allocating offices according to class (Pol. V 8, 1308b26).

In his view, this increases stability and prevents social unrest (which was frequent in Greek states). A broad middle class gives the state special stability (Pol. IV 11, 1295b25-38).

Poetics

"Poetry is finer and more philosophical than history; for poetry expresses the universal, and history only the particular." - Aristoteles

Theory of poetry

Mimêsis

The central concept of Aristotle's theory of poetry, which he elaborates in his *Poetics (poiêtikê), which was* not published during his lifetime, is *mimêsis,* that is, "imitation" or "representation." In addition to poetry in the narrower sense (epic, tragedy, comedy, and dithyrambic poetry), Aristotle also counts parts of music and dance among the mimetic arts (Poet. 1, 1447a).

Aristotle does not treat mimetic arts like painting and sculpture further, but only mentions that they also work according to the principle of imitation (Poet. 1, 1447a19 f.). Common to all mimetic arts is the temporal succession. In this respect, *mimêsis* can be understood as aesthetic action.

Aristotle sees in the pleasure of *mimêsis* a basic anthropological condition common to all human beings. For the pleasure in it as well as in its products is innate to humans, since they love to learn (Poet. 4, 1448b5-15).

Unlike the other mimetic arts, the use of language is specific to poetry. All poetry is, moreover, the representation of actions; not, however, of what has actually happened, but of "what could happen, that is, what is possible according to the rules of probability or necessity" (Poet. 9, 1451a37 f.). Depicted are actions that say something about man in general, not about random and arbitrary circumstances. The goal is not the imitation of people; it is not figures or characters that matter, but actions; the former are only means (Poet. 6, 1450a26-23).

Types seal

Aristotle classifies four forms of existing poetry according to two criteria: (i) the nature of the representation of action and (ii) the nature of the characters represented.

Dramatic representation is characterized by the fact that the respective character himself represents the action, reporting by the fact that the action is reported. By "better" and "worse" are meant the characters and their actions. Better figures or characters are somewhat better than ourselves, worse ones worse; neither, however, to the point where we can no longer identify with them (Poet. 5,

1449a31-1449b13). Aristotle's hypothesis here is that tragedy arose from epic and comedy from mocking song (Poet. 4, 1449a2-7).

Aristotle announces a study of the comedy. However, like the mocking song, it has not been handed down. He treats the epic quite briefly. His surviving theory of poetry is therefore primarily a theory of tragedy.

Tragedy

Aristotle defines tragedy as a This short sentence is one of the most discussed passages in all of Aristotle's work. (3) names the dramatic-performative element. (1) names (besides aspects already mentioned above) the (later so-called) unity of action. The unity of place and time was attributed to Aristotle's theory of tragedy in the Renaissance, but he himself did not advocate it in this way. (2) refers to the fact that the language of tragedy has melody and rhythm. By far the most attention has been given to (4), especially (4b).

Emotion arousal and catharsis

In (4) Aristotle describes the function of tragedy, what it should achieve. Largely undisputed is only(4a): The emotions of pity and fear should be aroused in the spectator by the depicted action.

It is unclear, however, whether *eleos* and *phobos* are actually to be rendered with "pity" and "fear" or with "elemental effects" "lamentation" and "shudder". That the action itself and not the performance plays the decisive role in the arousal of emotion is evident from the fact that Aristotle also considers the tragedy read by his theory. Pity is aroused when the protagonists suffer undeserved misfortune, fear when they resemble the spectator (or reader) in the process.

(4b) is highly controversial, since its mode of operation is not further explained. The word *catharsis,* which as a metaphor (like "purification" in German) has a surplus of meaning, has given rise to a wide variety of interpretations, especially because it was used even before Aristotle, namely in medicine (purification by emetics and laxatives) and in religious cults (purification of impure persons by religious practices), among others.

The grammatical construction purification *of the emotions* allows various interpretations as to what the purification consists of. Presumably, the emotions *themselves* are to be purified (by an emotion arousal); however, the statement has also been understood as purification of *the* emotions.

The normative-descriptive character of the theory of tragedy

Aristotle's theory of tragedy has two types of statements. On the one hand, he examines the foundations of poetry, distinguishes different types of it, and names parts of a tragedy and how it works. On the other hand, he also speaks of what a *good* tragedy is and what the poet *should* do accordingly. For example, he expresses that in a good tragedy, a protagonist does not go from good fortune to bad fortune because of either his good or bad character, but because of a mistake *(hamartia),* for example, like Oedipus because of ignorance.

Only a bad tragedy would show how a good character goes from happiness to unhappiness or a bad character goes from unhappiness to happiness. The reason for this is the function of tragedy, the evocation of pity and fear. In bad tragedies, pity and fear would not be aroused; in good ones, this is the case because of the nature of the protagonist and the fault as the cause of the misfortune (Poet. 13, 1452b28-1453a12).

Hymnos

Aristotle also wrote a hymn to Aretê in memory of his friend Hermias.

Reception

"History describes what has happened, poetry what might. Hence poetry is something more philosophic and serious than history; for poetry speaks of what is universal, history of what is particular." - Aristoteles

Ancient

Aristotle's teaching had far less influence on his school, the Peripatos, after his death than Plato's teaching had on his academy. Aristotle was not given a veneration comparable to that of Plato among the Platonists. On the one hand, this meant openness and flexibility, on the other hand, lack of cohesion based on content.

The Peripatetics devoted themselves primarily to empirical natural research and also dealt with ethics, the theory of the soul and the theory of the state, among other things. Aristotle's student Theophrastus, his successor as head of the school, and his successor Straton came to partly different results than the founder of the school. After Straton's death (270/268 BC), a period of decline began.

The study and commentary of Aristotle's writings was apparently neglected at that time in the Peripatos, at least far less eagerly pursued than the study of Plato in the competing Academy. It was not until the first century B.C. that Andronikos of Rhodes arranged for a compilation of Aristotle's doctrinal writings (Pragmatia), and there was also an upsurge in their interpretation by the Peripatetics.

The "exoteric" writings intended for the public, especially the dialogues, were popular for a long time, but were lost in the Roman imperial period. Cicero still knew them. The Peripatetics regarded the doctrinal writings as intended specifically for their internal teaching use. In the Roman imperial period, the most influential representative of Aristotelianism was Alexander of Aphrodisias, who argued against the Platonists on the mortality of the soul.

Although Aristotle had placed great emphasis on refuting core components of Platonism, it was the Neoplatonists who made a significant contribution to the preservation and dissemination of his legacy in late antiquity by adopting, commenting on, and integrating his logic into their system.

A particularly important role was played by Porphyrios in the 3rd century CE, Proclus in the 5th century, Ammonios Hermeiou (who established the tradition of Aristotle commentary in Alexandria), and Simplikios in the 6th century, who wrote important Aristotle commentaries.

In the 4th century, Themistios wrote paraphrases on works of Aristotle that achieved a strong after-effect. Among the commentators of late antiquity, he was the only Aristotelian (albeit one influenced by Neoplatonism); the others dealt with Aristotelianism from a Neoplatonic perspective, striving for a synthesis of Platonic and Aristotelian views, often showing a preponderance of the Platonic. As late as the beginning of the 7th century, the distinguished Christian philosopher Stephanos of Alexandria, who taught in Constantinople, commented on works by Aristotle.

Among the prominent ancient church fathers, Aristotle was little known and unpopular; some despised and mocked his dialectic. They resented the fact that he considered the universe uncreated and imperishable and doubted (or, according to their understanding, denied) the immortality of the soul. On the other hand, some Christian Gnostics and other heretical Christians had a more positive relationship with Aristotle: Arians (Aëtios, Eunomius), Monophysites, Pelagians and Nestorians - a circumstance that made the philosopher all the more suspect for the ecclesiastical authors. Syrians - Monophysites as well as Nestorians - translated the *Organon* into their language and dealt with it intensively.

In the 6th century, John Philoponus wrote Aristotle's commentaries, but also sharply criticized Aristotelian cosmology and physics. With his theory of impetus, he was a precursor of late medieval and early modern criticism of Aristotle's theory of motion.

Middle Ages

In the Byzantine Empire of the early Middle Ages, Aristotle was little respected. His influence was mainly indirect, namely through the mostly Neoplatonic-minded late antique authors, who had adopted parts of his teachings. Therefore, mixing with Neoplatonic thought was a given from the beginning. In John of Damascus, the Aristotelian component is clearly evident.

The 11th and 12th centuries saw a revival of interest in Aristotelian philosophy, with Michael Psellos, John Italos and his disciple Eustratios of Nikaia (both convicted of heresy), and the primarily philological Michael of Ephesus writing commentaries. The emperor's daughter Anna Komnena encouraged these efforts.

In the Islamic world, the impact of Aristotle's works began early and was broader and deeper than in late antiquity and in the early and high Middle Ages in Europe. Aristotelianism dominated qualitatively and quantitatively over the rest of the ancient tradition.

Already in the 9th century, most of Aristotle's works, often mediated by previous translation into Syriac (the first Syriac commentator on Aristotle was Sergios of Resaina), were available in Arabic, as were ancient commentaries. In addition, there was a rich body of spurious (pseudo-Aristotelian) writing, some of it of Neoplatonic content, including such writings as *the Theology of Aristotle* and the *Kalam fi mahd al-khair (Liber de causis)*.

Aristotelian ideas were mixed with Neoplatonic ones from the beginning, and there was a belief in a correspondence between the teachings of Plato and Aristotle. In this sense, al-Kindī (9th century) and al-Farabi (10th century) and the later tradition that followed them interpreted Aristotelianism; in ibn Sina (Avicenna), the Neoplatonic element came more to the fore. In contrast, a relatively pure Aristotelianism was represented in the 12th century by ibn Rušd (Averroes), who wrote numerous commentaries and defended Aristotelian philosophy against al-Ghazali.

In the Latin Middle Ages, only a small part of Aristotle's complete works was initially disseminated until the 12th century, namely two of the logical writings (*Categories* and *De interpretatione*) that Boethius had translated and annotated in the early 6th century, together with Porphyrios' Introduction to the Doctrine of Categories. This body of writing, later called the *Logica vetus*, formed the basis of the teaching of logic. With the great translation movement of the 12th and 13th centuries, this narrow limitation changed.

In the 12th century, the previously missing logical writings (*Analytica priora* and *posteriora, Topics, Sophistic Refutations*) became available in Latin; they made up the *Logica nova*. Then, one by one, almost all the remaining works became accessible (some only in the 13th century). Most of the writings were translated into Latin several times (either from Arabic or from Greek).

Michael Scotus translated Aristotle's commentaries of Averroes from Arabic. They were eagerly used, which led to the emergence of Latin Averroism in the second half of the 13th century, which was a relatively consistent Aristotelianism by the standards of the time.

In the course of the 13th century, Aristotle's writings, as standard textbooks, became the basis of scholastic science practiced at universities (in the Faculty of Liberal Arts); in 1255, his Logic, Natural Philosophy, and Ethics were prescribed as subject matter at this faculty of the University of Paris. The leading role was given to the Paris and Oxford Universities.

The Aristotle commentaries of Albertus Magnus were groundbreaking. Writing Aristotle's commentaries became a main occupation of the magisters, and many of them considered the annotated textbooks to be free of error. In addition to Aristotelian methodology, they studied the philosophy of science particularly intensively in order to use it as the basis for a hierarchically ordered system of the sciences.

However, resistance arose from the theological side against individual doctrines, especially against the theses of the eternity of the world and the absolute validity of the laws of nature (exclusion of miracles), as well as against Averroism. Therefore, in 1210, 1215, 1231, 1245, 1270 and 1277 there were ecclesiastical condemnations of doctrines and bans on Aristotle. However, they were directed only against the natural philosophical writings or against individual theses and could only temporarily inhibit the triumphant advance of Aristotelianism. These prohibitions only affected France (especially Paris), they did not apply in Oxford. Aristotle became "the philosopher" par excellence: with *Philosophus* (without addition) only he was meant, with *Commentator* Averroes. Opposing positions (especially in epistemology and anthropology) were held by followers of the Platonically influenced teachings of Augustine, especially Franciscans ("Franciscan school").

A prominent critic of Aristotelianism was the Franciscan Bonaventure. Another Franciscan, Petrus Johannis Olivi, stated disapprovingly around 1280: "He (Aristotle) is believed without reason - like a god of this age." Eventually, the Aristotelian system of doctrine (Thomism), modified and developed by the Dominican Thomas Aquinas, prevailed, first in his order and later throughout the Church.

However, people continued to wrongly attribute Neoplatonic writings to Aristotle, distorting the overall picture of his philosophy. Dante paid tribute to Aristotle's importance and reputation in his *Divine Comedy*, portraying him as a "master" admired and honored by the other ancient philosophers; however, Dante rejected some Aristotelian teachings.

Aristotle's *Politics* was first translated into Latin around 1260 by William of Moerbeke and then commented on and quoted by Thomas Aquinas and other scholastics. The justification of slavery or servitude in particular met with interest and fundamental approval among scholars. *Politics* stimulated commentators and authors of political treatises to discuss the advantages and disadvantages of hereditary or elective monarchy and of absolute or law-bound rule.

In the epoch of transition from the late Middle Ages to the early modern period, Nicholas of Cusa critically engaged with Aristotle. He imagined Aristotle as a fictitious interlocutor who could be made to understand the justification of the Cusanian doctrine of the *Coincidentia oppositorum,* although Aristotle should have rejected it according to his theorem of contradiction.

Modern times

"The roots of education are bitter, but the fruit is sweet."
- Aristoteles

During the Renaissance, humanists produced new translations of Aristotle into Latin that were much easier to read, so there was less reliance on the commentaries. The translations of the *Nicomachean Ethics* and the *Politics* by Leonardo Bruni, among others, are significant. However, people also began to read the original Greek texts. Fierce disputes arose between Platonists and Aristotelians, with the majority of the humanists involved leaning toward Plato.

However, there were also important Aristotelians in the Renaissance, such as Pietro Pomponazzi (1462-1525) and Jacopo Zabarella (1533-1589), and more commentaries on Aristotle were produced in the Occident at that time than during the entire Middle Ages. As in the Middle Ages, many Renaissance scholars still sought to reconcile Platonic and Aristotelian viewpoints with each other and with Catholic theology and anthropology.

However, since the 15th century, thanks to better access to the sources, it was possible to better understand the extent of the fundamental oppositions between Platonism, Aristotelianism and Catholicism. In communicating these insights, the Byzantine philosopher Georgios Gemistos Plethon played an important role. Independently, (neo)scholastic Aristotelianism, which continued the medieval tradition, continued to prevail with its method and terminology in schools and universities deep into modern times, even in Lutheran areas, although Martin Luther rejected Aristotelianism.

In the sixteenth century, Bernardino Telesio and Giordano Bruno made frontal attacks on Aristotelianism, and Petrus Ramus advocated a non-Aristotelian logic (Ramism). As early as 1554, Giovanni Battista Benedetti (1530-1590), in his work *Demonstratio proportionum motuum localium contra Aristotilem et omnes philosophos,* refuted in a simple thought experiment the Aristotelian assumption that bodies in free fall fall faster the heavier they are: Two equal spheres, firmly connected by a (massless) rod, fall with the same speed as each of the two spheres alone.

But it was not until the 17th century that a new understanding of science replaced the Aristotelian-

96

Scholastic tradition. The turnaround in physics was initiated by Galileo Galilei. In 1647, Aristotle's hypothesis of a horror vacui was refuted by Blaise Pascal with his experiment Emptiness in the Void. It was not until Isaac Newton's *Philosophiae Naturalis Principia Mathematica,* published in 1687, that a foundation of the new classical mechanics was established with the principle of inertia, which replaced the Aristotelian assumptions.

In biology, Aristotelian views were able to persist until the 18th century. In part, they proved fruitful. For example, William Harvey's discovery of the circulatory system was based on Aristotle's principle that nature produces nothing unnecessary, and he applied it to the nature of blood vessels and heart chambers, of which Aristotle mistakenly assumed three. Charles Darwin in 1879 called Aristotle "one of the greatest observers (if not the greatest) who ever lived."

The influence of Aristotle's *Poetics*, and in particular his theory of tragedy (→ Rule Drama), was very strong and enduring. It shaped the theory and practice of theater throughout the early modern period, with some weighty exceptions, especially in Spain and England (Shakespeare).

The *Poetics* had been available in Latin translation since 1278, and humanistic translations appeared in 1498 and 1536. The *poetics of* Julius Caesar Scaliger (1561), the poetry *doctrine* of Martin Opitz (1624), the French theater *doctrine* of the 17th century (*doctrine classique)* and finally the rule art demanded by Johann Christoph Gottsched (*Critische Dichtkunst,* 1730) were based on it.

In the 19th century, intensive philological study of Aristotle's work began, especially in Germany. In 1831, the complete edition commissioned by the Prussian Academy of Sciences and supervised by Immanuel Bekker was published. Hermann Bonitz wrote numerous translations and the *Index Aristotelicus, which* is still authoritative today.

At the end of the 19th century, the 15,000-page edition of the ancient Greek commentaries on Aristotle *(Commentaria in Aristotelem Graeca)* was published under the direction of Hermann Diels, also at the Berlin-based Academy.

As a result of the intensive philological debate, the long prevailing view that the Corpus Aristotelicum was a philosophical system composed as a whole was revised at the beginning of the 20th century, especially by Werner Jaeger. In the first half of the 20th century, modern Aristotelian research was dominated not only by Jaeger but also by W. D. Ross at Oxford; numerous students ensured an increasing preoccupation with Aristotle not only in the philological but also in the philosophical departments of Anglo-Saxon universities, which continues to this day.

Heidegger's analysis of being in fundamental ontology took place in intensive confrontation with Aristotle, which is also true for students like Hans Georg Gadamer. Aristotle had the greatest influence in the 20th century in ethics (virtue ethics) and political philosophy (in Germany especially in the school around Joachim Ritter, in the Anglo-Saxon area in communitarianism). In the second half of the 20th century, previously metaphysics-critical analytic philosophy took up Aristotle's substance theory explicitly (for example, David Wiggins: *Sameness and Substance,* the four-category ontology of Jonathan Lowe, or the ontology of Barry Smith) or his essentialism implicitly (e.g., Kripke).

The lunar crater Aristotle is named after him. The same is true for the asteroid (6123) Aristotle since 1995 and for the Aristotle Mountains in Grahamland on the Antarctic Peninsula since 2012.

Enjoy all our books for free…

Interesting biographies, engaging introductions, and more.

Join the exclusive United Library reviewers club!
You will get a new book delivered in your inbox every Friday.
Join us today, go to: https://campsite.bio/unitedlibrary

BOOKS BY UNITED LIBRARY
Kamala Harris: The biography
Barack Obama: The biography
Joe Biden: The biography
Adolf Hitler: The biography
Albert Einstein: The biography
Aristotle: The biography
Donald Trump: The biography
Marcus Aurelius: The biography
Napoleon Bonaparte: The biography
Nikola Tesla: The biography
Pope Benedict: The biography
Pope Francis: The biography

Bitcoin: An introduction to the world's leading cryptocurrency
And more…
See all our published books here:
https://campsite.bio/unitedlibrary

ABOUT UNITED LIBRARY
United Library is a small group of enthusiastic writers. Our goal is always to publish books that make a difference, and we are most concerned with whether a book will still be alive in the future. United Library is an independent company, founded in 2010, and now publishing around up to 50 books a year.

Joseph Bryan - FOUNDER/MANAGING EDITOR

Amy Patel - ARCHIVIST AND PUBLISHING ASSISTANT

Mary Kim - OPERATIONS MANAGER

Mary Brown - EDITOR AND TRANSLATOR

Terry Owen - EDITOR

Printed in the USA
CPSIA information can be obtained
at www.ICGtesting.com
LVHW011559210724
786101LV00014B/1198